A Beginning-to-Read Book

Spending and Saving

by Mary Lindeen

NORWOOD HOUSE PRESS

DEAR CAREGIVER, The *Beginning to Read—Read and Discover* books provide emergent readers the opportunity to explore the world through nonfiction while building early reading skills. The text integrates both common sight words and content vocabulary. These key words are featured on lists provided at the back of the book to help your child expand his or her sight word recognition, which helps build reading fluency. The content words expand vocabulary and support comprehension.

Nonfiction text is any text that is factual. The Common Core State Standards call for an increase in the amount of informational text reading among students. The Standards aim to promote college and career readiness among students. Preparation for college and career endeavors requires proficiency in reading complex informational texts in a variety of content areas. You can help your child build a foundation by introducing nonfiction early. To further support the CCSS, you will find Reading Reinforcement activities at the back of the book that are aligned to these Standards.

Above all, the most important part of the reading experience is to have fun and enjoy it!

Sincerely,

Shannon Cannon

Shannon Cannon, Ph.D.
Literacy Consultant

Norwood House Press
Chicago, Illinois
For more information about Norwood House Press please visit our website at www.norwoodhousepress.com or call 866-565-2900.
© 2020 Norwood House Press. Beginning-to-Read™ is a trademark of Norwood House Press. All rights reserved. No part of this book may be reproduced or utilized in any form or by any means without written permission from the publisher.

Editor: Judy Kentor Schmauss
Designer: Sara Radka

Photo Credits:
Getty Images, 1–3, 6–16, 20–23, 26–29; Shutterstock, 5, 17–19, 25

Library of Congress Cataloging-in-Publication Data
Names: Lindeen, Mary, author.
Title: Spending and saving / by Mary Lindeen.
Description: Chicago, Illinois : Norwood House Press, [2020] |
    Series: A beginning-to-read book | Audience: 5-8. | Audience: K to 3.
Identifiers: LCCN 2018054646 | ISBN 9781684509331 (hardcover) | ISBN
    9781684044351 (pbk.) | ISBN 9781684044405 (ebook)
Subjects: LCSH: Money-Juvenile literature. | Savings accounts-Juvenile literature. |
    Consumption (Economics)-Juvenile literature.
Classification: LCC HG221.5 .L45 2020 | DDC 332-dc23
LC record available at https://lccn.loc.gov/2018054646

Hardcover ISBN: 978-1-68450-933-1
Paperback ISBN: 978-1-68404-435-1

Look at all of these people.
They are working hard!

People earn
money when
they work.

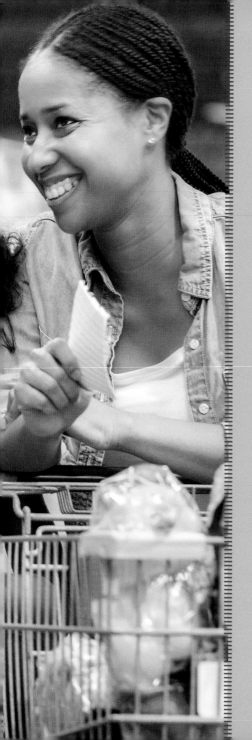

They can spend
their money to buy
things they need.

They can also
spend it to buy
things they want.

When people
spend their money,
it's gone.

They don't have
it anymore.

That's why people
often choose
to save some
of their money.

They keep it
for a while
instead of
spending it
right away.

People who save money
usually put it in a bank.

Some banks are big.

And some are small.

People can save a little
money or a lot of money.

They can save money for a
short time or a long time.

People save for things they need to have.

And they save for things
they want to have.

People save for things they need to do.

And they save for things they want to do.

People also save for emergencies.

They save for special occasions, too.

When people
spend their
savings, they take
it out of the bank.

Then they can
spend the money
they saved.

And then they can start saving all over again!

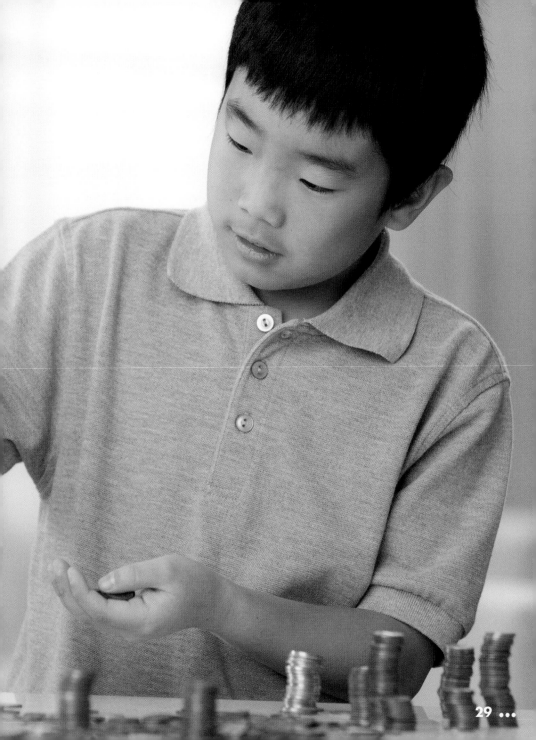

...READING REINFORCEMENT...

CRAFT AND STRUCTURE

To check your child's understanding of this book, recreate the following chart on a sheet of paper. Read the book with your child, and then help him or her identify the main idea of the book and several details that tell about the main idea.

MAIN IDEA:	
Detail 1:	
Detail 2:	
Detail 3:	
Detail 4:	

VOCABULARY: Learning Content Words

Content words are words that are specific to a particular topic. All of the content words in this book can be found on page 32. Use some or all of these content words to complete one or more of the following activities:

- Ask your child to act out the meanings of the words as you guess the word being acted out. Switch roles.

- Help your child make word associations, i.e., *What are two words that go together? Why?*

- Provide your child with several clues as to the meaning of the words and ask him or her to guess which word you're thinking of.

- Write the words on slips of paper and put them in a hat or container. Ask your child to pick a word and use it in a sentence.

- Write the words, scrambling the letters. Provide a definition of the word, have your child guess the word, and then unscramble the letters.

FOUNDATIONAL SKILLS: Pronouns

Pronouns are words used in place of nouns (people, places, things, or ideas). Have your child identify which words are pronouns in the list below. Then help your child find pronouns in this book.

save	help	we	fog
me	Charlie	it	why
you	they	our	he

CLOSE READING OF INFORMATIONAL TEXT

Close reading helps children comprehend text. It includes reading a text, discussing it with others, and answering questions about it. Use these questions to discuss this book with your child:

- How do people earn money?
- Why do people save money?
- Where is a good place to put money you are saving? Why?
- What is an example of something you might spend money on?
- What happens when you spend all the money you have?
- Do you think it's important to save money? Why or why not?

FLUENCY

Fluency is the ability to read accurately with speed and expression. Help your child practice fluency by using one or more of the following activities:

- Reread the book to your child at least two times while he or she uses a finger to track each word as it is read.
- Read a line of the book, then reread it as your child reads along with you.
- Ask your child to go back through the book and read the words he or she knows.
- Have your child practice reading the book several times to improve accuracy, rate, and expression.

··· Word List ···

Spending and Saving uses the 68 words listed below. *High-frequency words* are those words that are used most often in the English language. They are sometimes referred to as sight words because children need to learn to recognize them automatically when they read. *Content words* are any words specific to a particular topic. Regular practice reading these words will enhance your child's ability to read with greater fluency and comprehension.

High-Frequency Words

a	can	of	small	time
again	do	often	some	to
all	for	or	take	too
also	have	out	the	want
and	in	over	their	when
are	it	people	then	while
at	little	put	these	who
away	long	right	they	why
big	look	save	things	work(ing)

Content Words

anymore	earn	it's	occasions	start
bank(s)	emergencies	keep	save(ed, ing, s)	that's
buy	gone	lot	short	usually
choose	hard	money	special	
don't	instead	need	spend(ing)	

··· About the Author

Mary Lindeen is a writer, editor, parent, and former elementary school teacher. She has written more than 100 books for children and edited many more. She specializes in early literacy instruction and books for young readers, especially nonfiction.